How to Improve Your Child's
LANGUAGE &
THINKING SKILLS

by Florence Karnofsky and Trudy Weiss

Fearon Teacher Aids
A Division of Frank Schaffer Publications, Inc.

This Fearon Teacher Aids product was formerly manufactured and distributed by American Teaching Aids, Inc., a subsidiary of Silver Burdett Ginn, and is now manufactured and distributed by Frank Schaffer Publications, Inc. FEARON, FEARON TEACHER AIDS, and the FEARON balloon logo are marks used under license from Simon & Schuster, Inc.

Editorial Director: Virginia L. Murphy
Editor: Virginia Massey Bell
Copyeditor: Kristin Eclov
Cover Design: Lucyna Green
Design: Teena Remer

ISBN 0-86653-931-X

Printed in the United States of America

1.987

Acknowledgments

Illustrations in this book were drawn by the children at Nathan Hale Elementary School in Lansing, Illinois. A special thanks to Benjamin Weiss for his drawings on pages 28, 35, and 72, Becky Jane Wilk for drawings on pages 5-7, 13, 19, and 42, and Justin Wilk for his drawings on pages 1 and 4.

We would like to thank Dr. David Peal for his invaluable advice in preparing this book.

We'd also like to acknowledge the following for his suggestions:

William S. Edmunds
Retired Principal and Reading Specialist
Talala Elementary School
Park Forest, IL

Dedication

This book is dedicated to the many children who taught us so much over the years.

About the Authors

Trudy Weiss spent eighteen years teaching
in grades one through eight, two years
as a teacher of learning disabled children,
and three years as a curriculum coordinator.
She has also coauthored several articles
for several teacher magazines.

Florence Karnofsky has taught elementary children
in Indiana and Pennsylvania for twenty-five years,
specializing in the areas of science and social studies.

CONTENTS

INTRODUCTION

• • • • • • • • • • • • • • • •

HOW THIS BOOK CAN HELP YOU

This book is designed to help your child do better in school by improving his or her language and thinking skills. The simple methods we describe here can help your child learn to read more easily and to understand social studies, science, and math better, resulting in improved grades in school.

Our methods are neither mysterious, nor time-consuming. There's no expensive computer to buy and you do not have to spend hours and hours drilling your child. You need only become aware of some simple techniques that will make it easier for your child to learn in school.

Take every opportunity to talk with your child. Talking together is a great opportunity to expand your child's vocabulary and improve his or her language skills. Encourage your child to ask questions, to make decisions, and to enjoy reading books with you, as well as independently. To help you, we have included vocabulary suggestions by category, a synonym dictionary, and a number of games to play with your child.

It's never too early or too late to help your child learn. The methods we describe in this book work with toddlers and preschoolers, as well as children in school who are having difficulty. The child who is already doing well in school will also benefit.

After 25 years of talking with parents, we can truthfully say we have never met a parent who was not eager to help his or her child do better in school. *How to Improve Your Child's Language & Thinking Skills* contains the advice we have given to parents of the children we have taught over the years. These parents have told us how these suggestions helped them and we believe they will help you, too.

CHAPTER 1
HOW ONE WORD MAKES A DIFFERENCE

Let's suppose Dad and six-year-old Stanley have arrived downtown for a dentist appointment. As they walk to the dentist's office, they pass a construction site where a new building is being completed. Here are two ways Dad might describe the building-in-progress to Stan:

"Stan, look at that big building."

"Stan, look at that new office building under construction."

In the first example, Stan already understands the word "big" and has learned nothing new. In the second sentence, by using "office" instead of "big," and including the words "under construction," Dad added new words to Stan's vocabulary. He created an opportunity to talk about different types of buildings, occupations, and building methods.

As they talked, Stan learned that an office is a place where doctors, lawyers, dentists, typists, secretaries, and sales representatives work. He learned it's a place where businesses, such as computer companies and banks, have their offices. Stan also learned that when something is being built, it is "under construction." Dad gave Stan the opportunity to ask questions about what he saw. This approach encouraged Stan to find out more information about the world around him.

Dad didn't try to teach or preach and Stan did not have to understand every word Dad said. In time, through more conversations like this one, Stan will become more knowledgeable.

One day, Stan may come across the words "office" and "under construction." He may hear his teacher use the word "office" when talking about the principal or the school administration. Stan's teacher may ask Stan to take something to the office or he may come across the word in his social studies text or spelling book. Or, Stan's teacher may refer to a street or sidewalk in the neighborhood that is "under construction." Stan will soon learn that the term "under construction" is not limited to buildings-in-progress, but can include anything that is being built, such as bridges, playgrounds, houses, and so on. Stan is fortunate. Because Dad talked to Stan about office buildings and buildings under construction, Stan now understands these concepts and may recognize these words later should they appear in class discussion or his classroom reading materials.

● ● ● ● ● ● ● ● ● ●

WHAT STANLEY LEARNED FROM TALKING WITH DAD

1. A category of buildings called *office buildings*

2. The variety of occupations of people in office buildings

3. Tall buildings often contain offices for a variety of companies

4. A building that is being built is "under construction"

5. There are a variety of jobs involved in construction

6. There are a variety of different ways to construct buildings

● ● ● ● ● ● ● ● ● ●

HOW MANY WORDS SHOULD YOUR CHILD KNOW?

The average adult knows between 30,000 and 40,000 words, but actively uses about 10,000. On average, children entering school have a vocabulary of about 4,000 words. It is believed that children who are exposed to a greater quantity and variety of words will have larger vocabularies and be better prepared for school.

In many schools, children are given intelligence tests, which have several parts. One part is a vocabulary test in which the children are asked to give the meanings of words. The other sections measure a child's ability to see relationships and to remember and understand concepts. Children who have large vocabularies usually score higher on mental ability tests than those with limited vocabularies.

Today, psychologists recognize that intelligence contains multiple facets not measured by mental ability tests. They accept, however, that children who score well on traditional mental ability tests are more likely to succeed in school than those who score poorly. Many psychologists also agree that a child's mental ability is not fixed at birth, but can be raised through the stimulation of play, conversation, reading, being read to, as well as other challenging experiences.

A child learns words from playmates, television, family, and friends, but most words are learned from listening to parents. When Mother coos to newly born Mira, "You're beautiful," she begins the process of teaching Mira new words. Mira doesn't understand her mother on that first day, but before her first birthday, Mira will have learned the words for "daddy," "mommy," "wet," "cold," "sleepy," "hungry," "strong," and "bottle," among others.

WHAT WORDS SHOULD YOU USE?

When talking to children, it is natural to try to simplify conversations. Children, however, can learn more words than we think. For example, a five-year-old playing with blocks was overheard saying, "Here comes the demolition crew. They're going to jack up the floor." The child learned these new words from a home-repair show on television.

The following are examples of how you can use words to increase your child's vocabulary:

Mira (age 3): Daddy, look at my picture.

Daddy: It's beautiful. We'll hang it on the refrigerator.

Mira is happy. Daddy praised her. She's pleased with him and herself. However, there's more that Dad can do to expand Mira's vocabulary and experience with words.

Mira: Daddy, look at my picture.

Dad: Mira, that's a lovely picture. It's very colorful. Where shall we hang it?

Mira: On the refrigerator.

Dad: Great idea! We will call the refrigerator door Mira's Art Gallery. We'll put all your pictures in your gallery.

Sample Suggested Words to Use with Young Children When Describing Artwork

humorous	imaginative	thoughtful
lively	attractive	fanciful
joyful	mysterious	sunny

Sample Suggested Words to Use with Older Children When Describing Artwork

clever	balanced	original
graceful	expressive	detailed
stark	realistic	abstract

By taking advantage of daily experiences to introduce new words, you are increasing your child's vocabulary. Within a few years, Mira's vocabulary will expand to a substantial pre-kindergarten level of 5,000 to 6,000 words.

THE STORY OF HOW GRANDPA OVERDID IT

Grandpa, Grandma, and Sarah, age 8, were on vacation driving across the state of Arizona.

Grandpa: Look, Sarah. Do you see how the telephone wire hangs in a curve between the two poles? That shape is called "a catenary."

Grandpa: (A minute later.) Look, Sarah, how that mountain overlays this other one. That's called "a thrust fault."

Grandma: George, school is over for the summer.

Sarah is relieved and silently thanks Grandma for stopping Grandpa's many lessons.

Although Grandpa's intentions were good, he overdid it. In his enthusiasm, he made every word a vocabulary lesson, and Sarah was turned off by the whole experience. Grandpa would have been wiser to introduce words in a more natural way. For example, suppose Grandpa is getting breakfast for Sarah. The conversation might develop in this way:

Grandpa: Here's the cereal selection for today. You can have shredded wheat, bran cereal, or cornflakes. Sarah, which do you want?

Sarah: Shredded wheat for me. Bran...yuck!

Grandpa: OK, shredded wheat for Sarah. Do you know what bran is, Sarah?

Sarah: Nope.

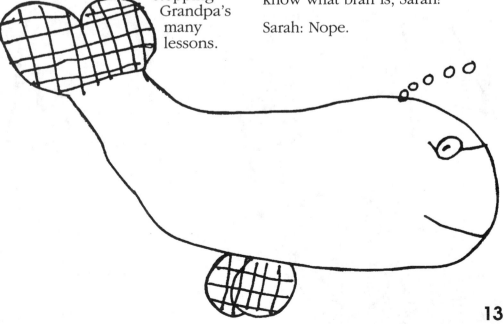

13

Grandpa: Bran is the outside shell of a grain. Bran is like the skin around a peanut. Only it's the skin around the shell of a grain like wheat, rye, or oats.

This time instead of giving Sarah a lecture, Grandpa introduced new words in a natural way. As a result, good things happened:

1. Grandpa accepted Sarah's distaste for bran, but used the opportunity to teach her what bran was.

2. He also introduced Sarah to these new words—grain, wheat, rye, and oats.

Sarah won't remember everything Grandpa has told her, but tomorrow when she sees the same cereal boxes on the table, she'll probably recall that bran is like the skin of a peanut around a grain. If Grandpa uses bran, grain, wheat, and so on a few more times, Sarah will become more familiar with these terms. In addition to

seeing these words on the cereal boxes every morning, Sarah will also hear the words used in television commercials. Eventually, these same words will turn up in a social studies, health, reading, science, or spelling lesson. Sarah will be familiar with these words and will have a good understanding of what they mean.

HOW ONE WORD MAKES A DIFFERENCE

Remember that slight changes in what you say to your child can make an enormous difference in the size of your child's vocabulary. Here are some examples.

Instead of:	Say:
Put your arm in your sleeve.	Put your right arm in your right sleeve.
I'll cut your apple.	I'll cut your apple into several small sections.
Your pants are too short.	Your pants are two inches too short.
We are almost there.	We only have a mile to go and we'll be there.
Look at the water.	Look at the little pond.

Bedtime, travel time, television time, eating time, driving time—they are all good times to teach your child new words. It is important to use every opportunity to introduce your child to new vocabulary. The more familiar your child is with the spoken language, the better prepared he or she will be for success in school.

CHAPTER 2
HOW CHILDREN BECOME BETTER READERS

Mom was reading four-year-old Ben's favorite story, *Curious George*. In the middle of the story, Ben said, "I want to read," and much to his mom's surprise, Ben finished reading the story aloud without missing a word. As the days passed, Mom was pleased to see Ben recognizing more and more words on cereal boxes, signs, and other printed material.

"Can you believe it? Ben can read," she told the next door neighbor. "I wonder how he learned."

HOW DID BEN TEACH HIMSELF TO RECOGNIZE WORDS?

Ben learned to recognize words in books that were read to him over and over again. For example, after seeing the word "cat" dozens of times, he began to recognize the shape of the word. A picture of a cat accompanying the printed word helped Ben remember that c-a-t spelled cat.

Ben's mom never sat down deliberately to teach him how to read. He learned because Mom provided an environment that was conducive to learning. The kinds of things she did, such as reading to him, visits to the library, and so on, starting from Ben's birth and continuing throughout his elementary school years, helped Ben to become a better reader.

MOM'S EFFORTS MADE A DIFFERENCE

Ben's Mom Took the Time to Talk to Him

The surest way to teach children to understand language is to talk to them. This takes time and patience.

When children hear language spoken over and over again in association with experiences, they begin to understand the meanings of the words and sentences.

For example, Ben, age 4, is at the store with his mom buying some new clothes:

Mom: Which pair of jeans should we buy—the brown ones or the blue ones?

Ben: The blue ones.

Mom: Now let's choose a shirt to go with the jeans. Do you see a shirt that you like?

Ben: I don't know.

Mom: Let's put some shirts by the jeans and maybe you can tell which one you like best.

Ben: This one.

Through this simple conversation, Mom involved Ben in language and introduced him to several new words. She also gave Ben an opportunity to make choices that involved thinking. By expanding his vocabulary and encouraging Ben to think, Mom is preparing Ben to learn to read.

Ben, at age 10, is sitting on the front steps of his house talking with his grandpa.

Grandpa: Who do you think is going to win the National League championship, Ben?

Ben: The Pirates.

Grandpa: What makes you pick the Pirates?

Ben: They have the best players. They have Bonilla, Bond, and Andy Van Slyke.

Grandpa: That's true, but the Braves have good players, too. I think it's a matter of luck.

Ben: No, it isn't luck. Bonilla batted in 100 runs. Who do the Braves have that can do that?

Grandpa: But it takes more than two or three outfielders to make a winning team. What about the pitchers, the catcher, and the infield?

Ben: Sure, you need all the players, but the Pirates have the superstars, so they'll win.

Grandpa took time for a give-and-take conversation with Ben. He countered Ben's ideas with questions and statements that caused Ben to formulate and express his opinions. The more Ben participates in oral conversations of this type, the better he will understand language on the printed page.

The idea that parents should talk to their children seems so obvious that parents are apt not to recognize how important talking is to the learning process.

Ben's Mom Talked About Everything

From the day he was born, Ben's mom talked to him about everyday things she was doing and thinking. She used a variety of words, involved Ben in conversations, and encouraged thinking. The following are some examples of what parents can do to increase their child's vocabulary:

If you're working on the computer, explain to your child each step of what you are doing.

If you're washing clothes, discuss why you separate clothes into bundles, what the dials on the washer indicate, why you use pre-wash, and so on.

If you're thinking about whether to get new tires for your car, express your thoughts aloud to your child. If you are driving to buy tires, talk about the choices you have and encourage your child's responses.

If you're planning a garden, explain what kind of flowers or vegetables you would like to grow and ask for your child's assistance in choosing plant varieties.

If you're planning a vacation, explain to your child the variety of sites to see and the schedule you need to follow. Encourage your child to help in making decisions about the trip itinerary.

Ben's Mom Used the Appropriate Word

Parents sometimes avoid using the appropriate word needed for a specific situation. They assume their child will not be able to pronounce the word or understand its meaning. Sometimes baby talk seems "cute." But baby talk is of no value to a child who is learning to read. Children need to be challenged to learn new words, rather than using words that are familiar and overused. Textbooks in the elementary schools are sometimes written in language that is more advanced than the experiences and vocabularies of many children. Your child needs all the experience he or she can get with new and appropriate unfamiliar words.

Here are some examples of words found in a second-grade textbook:

amazement	astonishment	cleaver	crouched
cruise	drainage	dungeon	galley
impression	musket	provisions	urge
pouch	tinderbox	vault	ventured

These are words found in a fifth-grade textbook:

anti-toxin	anvil	appease	apprentice
atmosphere	brandish	buoy	cavalcade
chastise	exult	implore	myriad
penance	sextant	sullen	undaunted

Teachers are continually trying to challenge children to learn new vocabulary words, but it is important to expose children to a variety of new words at home, too. Children become more familiar with words after hearing them used several times. Ideally, it would be helpful to reinforce the vocabulary practice your child is getting at school by using the same vocabulary words in your conversations at home.

Mom Read to Ben

*There is no frigate
like a book to take us
lands away...*

*Books are keys to
wisdom's treasure;*

*Books are gates to
lands of pleasure.*

Ben's mom began reading
to him when he was six
months old and continued
to read hundreds of books
to him until he preferred
to read independently.
Unfortunately, some parents
read only an occasional
book to their children—
and some parents don't read
to their children at all.

Research tells us that children who have
exposure to many
newspapers, magazines,
encyclopedias, almanacs,
fiction and non-fiction
books in their homes, as
well as see their
parents read-
ing regularly,
score better on reading tests
than children who do not.

Parents read to their children
primarily to share the joy that
is found in books. But, in
fact, they are accomplishing
much more. Through books,
parents introduce their
children to hundreds of
new ideas they would not
otherwise have learned
about. Because children
listen so intently, they often
learn new words from the
context of a story. Books
also stimulate the
imagination and increase
the comprehension of lan-
guage. The simplest bedtime
fairy tale contains a host
of new vocabulary words
and concepts unfamiliar
to a young child.

Here are examples of words from *Little Red Riding Hood:*

hood	forest	fairy
fairy tale	imagination	thoughtful
carpenter	frightening	cottage
woods	ravenous	heed
wary	sly	bedridden

Children who are exposed to an assortment of reading materials, such as fairy tales, alphabet books, stories, and so on, are introduced to a variety of new words. Each time a book or story is reread, the vocabulary words and their meanings are reinforced.

Mom Played with Ben

When Ben was three, Mom bought him a large bag of sturdy, wooden blocks. While Ben built towers, bridges, and laid roadways and airplane runways, Mom made occasional suggestions and supplied words that named his many constructions. When Ben played by himself or with other children, he used the words he learned from Mom. Knowing a variety of vocabulary words stimulated Ben's imagination and helped him to plan and make decisions. As Ben grew older, Mom joined him in playing board games and some outdoor sports as well. Playing or free time is a good time to expand a child's vocabulary. The relaxed atmosphere encourages conversation and new concepts can be introduced in a natural way. Mom's involvement with Ben highly increased his vocabulary, which will be helpful to Ben later in school.

Ben's Mom Watched Television with Ben

Mom often watched television with Ben. During the commercials, she encouraged him to express his observations and opinions of what they were viewing. The programs and commercials provided subjects to talk about and the pictures reinforced the topics of their discussions.

When children view television alone, the experience can sometimes be worthwhile. With the addition of family talks, children's vocabularies expand and their under-standing of their world develops. What children learn from television and their family discussions can help them better understand their textbooks in reading, social studies, science, English, math, and health.

Ben's Mom Encouraged Ben

"The sweetest of all words is praise."

While Grandpa and Ben were driving to the grocery store, Ben saw a steel transmission tower.

Ben: Look, Grandpa. That's a pylon.

Grandpa: You're right, Ben. So it is. That's a pretty good word for a five-year-old to know. Where did you learn it?

Ben: Mom told me. Look, Grandpa! There's another pylon.

When Ben used a new word or expressed an idea that had previously been

23

explained to him, Mom always complimented his efforts. During Ben's first four years, Mom talked and read to Ben, played and watched television with him, and praised him for his accomplishments. Not only did she teach him new words, but she provided a wealth of experiences that added to Ben's comprehension and understanding.

discuss what is happening on the program or commercial. Praise your child for the gains he or she makes in learning new words and in asking questions about things he or she doesn't understand.

HOW TO PREPARE THE WAY FOR GREATER SUCCESS IN SCHOOL

Take time to talk to your child about everything. Use words that expand your child's vocabulary and general knowledge about the world. Read to your child and play with him or her. Always talk about what you are playing or reading. Watch television together and

CHAPTER 3
TEACHING YOUR CHILD TO THINK

Mother: Kevin, you're not thinking!

Teacher: Kevin, now stop and think!

Dad: Kevin, don't you ever think?

Sister: Kevin! Who do you think you are?

WHAT IS "THINKING"?

Poor Kevin! Everybody is picking on him. People are always saying he doesn't think. "But I am thinking," Kevin tells himself. "What do they expect?"

Kevin is honest when he says he doesn't know what people expect.

Mr. Baca expects the children in his class to do more than memorize in school. He wants them to think. The children in his class, including Kevin, are studying the life of people who live in desert countries. They are looking at a color slide of three men sitting in an oasis surrounded by palm trees. Seven camels with packs on their backs are grazing nearby.

Mr. Baca: Kevin, how do you think these men in the oasis might earn their living?

Kevin: I don't know.

Tony: Maybe they grow something in the oasis, then they pick it, then they get on their camels and go some place to sell it.

Mr. Baca: Good, Tony. You studied the picture carefully.

(Kevin thinks to himself, "He's smarter than me.")

Kevin couldn't answer Mr. Baca's question because Kevin saw just a picture of a few men with some camels. Kevin feels uneasy about answering questions that begin with "What do you think?"

Tony, on the other hand, feels at ease because starting from the time he could talk, his parents, through their normal conversations, encouraged him to think by asking him questions or asking him for his opinion.

Here are some examples of conversations between parents and children that stimulate thinking.

A conversation between Mother and Molly, age 3:

Mother: Do you think you want to eat stew or a sandwich for lunch?

Molly: Stew.

Mother: Can you hand me a dish for the stew?

Molly chooses a plate.

Mother: That's a nice plate, Molly. It's good for a sandwich. Which dish is good for something soupy like this stew?

Through this simple conversation, Molly gets practice in:

1. Observing several dishes and making a choice

2. Comparing shapes to find something good for stew

3. Learning to distinguish between plates and bowls

Conversation between Dad and Willie, Age 5:

Dad: Willie, your birthday is coming up. What should we do to get ready for your birthday party?

Willie: Buy some presents.

Dad (smiling): Of course. But if you're having a party, what should we do first?

Willie: Invite my friends.

Dad: Good idea. Who should we invite to the party?

Through this conversation, Dad gave Willie opportunities for thinking about:

1. Arranging events in sequence and considering the facts

2. Decision-making. Because Willie is young, Dad guided him in making an appropriate decision

A conversation with Dad and Jamal, age 8:

Dad: Why do you think we have to water the grass, Jamal?

Jamal: It'll die if we don't.

Dad: But why?

Jamal: It'll dry up.

Dad: Why do we keep watering the grass after we can see that it is wet?

Jamal: To wet the ground.

Dad: That's right. Why does the ground need to get wet?

Jamal: So the roots can soak up more water?

Dad: Absolutely right.

In this conversation, through casual questioning, Dad gave Jamal thinking practice in:

1. Observing and answering "why" questions

2. Putting observations in logical order

3. Being pressed to think further

FIVE THINKING SKILLS FOR YOUNG CHILDREN

1. To observe details and report them

2. To compare and contrast what is observed

3. To arrange facts into groups

4. To arrange facts into logical order

5. To form conclusions

TYPICAL SCHOOL ASSIGNMENTS THAT REQUIRE THINKING

Primary Teacher: There are ten pictures of animals on the bulletin board. The names are printed underneath each picture. On your paper, print the names of the animals in two groups. The first group should be animals with fur. The second group should be animals with feathers.

Intermediate Teacher: Your assignment today is to write a story describing how the people in this picture earn a living and explain why you think their life is harder or easier than yours.

Primary Teacher: First, experiment with your magnets. Then decide which items the magnet attracts and think about how these items are alike.

Intermediate Teacher: We have been studying about lower and higher forms of life. Your assignment today is to pick an animal that interests you. Then make a list of topics you want to investigate.

In each of these examples, the children are required to make decisions. In order to make good decisions, children must think about their choices.

WHEN SHOULD YOU BEGIN ENCOURAGING YOUR CHILD TO THINK?

Children should be stimulated to think as soon they are able to talk. Simply remember to ask questions that begin with "why," "what," "when," "where," "who," and "how."

Talk about every aspect of your daily life in a natural, encouraging way. This will help develop both language skills and thinking, which, as stated earlier, are important to learning to read—a factor in earning good grades in school.

SIX WAYS TO STIMULATE THINKING (AND DEVELOP LANGUAGE SKILLS)

1. Ask questions that have more than one correct answer.

Example: Why do you think that team won the game?

2. Avoid questions that can be answered with only one word.

Example: Did you have a good time at the party?
Instead: Tell me about the birthday party.

3. Encourage your child to expand his or her answer.

Example: Which cartoon do you like best? Why?

4. When a child answers a question poorly, avoid saying, "No, You're wrong," or "That's dumb." Instead, say "Can you think of another possible reason?" or "I hadn't thought about that. Let's think about that some more."

5. Give your child choices that require thinking.

Example: What should we buy Stephanie for her birthday?

6. Ask your child's opinion on family decisions.

Examples: Where should we go for dinner?
What program should we watch on television? What do you think we should plant in the vegetable garden?

THINKING TURN-OFFS

1. "Don't ask so many questions."
2. "You're too young to ask questions."
3. "I don't have time right now."

THINKING TURN-ONS

1. "Good question."
2. "You were pretty smart to think of that."
3. "That's an interesting idea you have there."

THINKING AND DEVELOPING LANGUAGE THROUGH TALKING

Whenever you ask your child thought-provoking questions, you are developing his or her thinking skills. Since your child will respond by talking, he or she will also be developing language skills. Your child will also be organizing his or her thoughts, as well as choosing words to express his or her beliefs and opinions. These are good opportunities for you to introduce new vocabulary. Thinking and developing language skills often go hand-in-hand. We have provided you with several simple suggestions for improving your child's thinking and language skills on the pages that follow.

For Ages 3 to 5

1. Ask your child to compare a dog with a cat, a tree with a bush, grass with weeds, a horse with a cow.

2. Ask your child to look at a picture and tell what's in it.

3. Ask your child to tell you what he or she saw on television.

4. Ask your child to name different items of clothing.

5. Ask your child to tell how a car and an airplane are alike and different.

6. Plant a seed or bean in a pot. Observe and discuss its growth every other day.

7. Ask your child which objects are his or hers and which ones are yours.

8. Ask your child which toys he or she thinks should be shared and which ones shouldn't.

9. Ask your child why it is necessary to wear a seat belt.

10. Talk about the different types of buildings and trees on your street.

11. Ask your child to compare the papa bear, the mama bear, and the little baby bear in the story *The Three Bears*.

12. Discuss with your child your activities for the morning.

13. When preparing for a shopping trip, discuss what you are going to do first, second, and so on.

14. When driving home, discuss what you are going to do when you arrive home.

For Ages 6 to 10

1. Ask what your child saw on the way home from school.

2. Ask what subjects in school your child likes and why.

3. Discuss how to re-arrange your child's room or the clothes in a drawer.

4. Ask your child to look at the clouds and notice how they are different on different days.

5. Ask what are fair punishments for poor behavior.

6. Ask what driving rules people are following on the road.

7. Ask your child to explain how children differ from one another. Ask how families differ.

8. Ask your child to compare the characters Goldilocks and Cinderella.

9. Ask your child to compare spring and fall or Christmas and Halloween.

10. Discuss the seasons of the year and the changes that occur.

11. Ask your child to tell how he or she is going to spend the morning at school.

12. Discuss the directions for playing a game.

CHAPTER 4
BETTER GRADES IN SOCIAL STUDIES

At age 10, Zubin Agarwal, newly arrived from India, entered fourth grade in an American school. The children were studying about the Revolutionary War. Poor Zubin! Although he spoke English quite well, he had never heard of George Washington, the Fourth of July, or the Declaration of Independence. He did not know about pilgrims, Native Americans, Columbus, and Thanksgiving. Zubin did not know words that his classmates had learned before they entered school. Bright as he was, Zubin lacked the vocabulary to understand his social studies assignments.

WHAT IS SOCIAL STUDIES?

Years ago, schools taught geography and history as separate subjects. Today, the two are combined into a subject called social studies, which includes sociology (how people live in groups), anthropology (how people live in different societies), and economics (how people work, use money, and buy and sell goods and services). Not a day goes by that you don't teach social studies in your home. You are teaching your child social studies if you talk about:

religion
how nations differ
presidents
Congress
elections
Native Americans
Afro-Americans
Asians
banks
your work
other people's jobs
battleships
airports
railroads
skyscrapers
lakes
mountains
oceans
deserts
current events

Our perception of social studies has changed over the years. Every time you discuss the events occurring in your neighborhood, community, country, family, or world, you are teaching your child about social studies. You can open your child's view of the world by pointing out on a globe the countries where certain products come from, or show your child the country where a particular endangered species lives. Social studies offers opportunities to talk with your child about a variety of subjects, thus expanding his or her vocabulary and ability to think.

HOW CHILDREN LEARN SOCIAL STUDIES FROM THEIR PARENTS

In the natural course of your daily life, you are teaching your child social studies when you:

Take your child to see parades on national holidays and explain what the nation is celebrating.

Fly a flag in front of your house and explain what it represents.

Talk about an approaching election.

Discuss the origin of certain foods and inventions, such as ice cream and the printing press.

OPPORTUNITIES FOR LEARNING SOCIAL STUDIES

Children learn social studies when they travel, go to museums, and watch television programs with a social-studies content. They learn from reading books about the past and about foreign countries. If children earn a small allowance, they learn about the value of money. When children hear the family discussing the news or looking at newspapers and magazines that come into their homes, they are learning about current events. Children who have been introduced to social studies through such experiences, have an enormous vocabulary and comprehension advantage over children who have not had these same opportunities.

WHAT YOU CAN DO FOR YOUR CHILD

If, after reading the preceding paragraph, you feel you have neglected your child's social studies education, you shouldn't feel guilty. You don't have to buy a set of encyclopedias, take trips, and go to museums every Saturday morning to improve your child's social studies skills. Here are several worthwhile suggestions for helping your child achieve better grades in social studies classes in school.

experience. Examples include:

family matters	religion
money	places to visit
holidays	your ancestors
foods	telephones
your childhood	elections
races of people	prejudices
your town	corporations
types of work	advertising
government	transportation
sports	ethnic groups
unemployment	taxes
government	television
farming	manufacturing
mining	boats
airlines	newspapers
famous people	foreign countries

EASY WAYS TO HELP YOUR CHILD

1. The most important thing you can do is talk to your child about every subject within his or her

2. Tack a large calendar on the wall near your child's bed. Discuss and record on the calendar a variety of events, such as:

dental appointments
family birthdays
school opening
school holidays
Lincoln's birthday
Washington's birthday
Martin Luther King, Jr., Day
Veterans Day
ethnic holidays
family celebrations
vacation days
important news events

3. While writing these events on the calendar, talk about them with your child—using as many appropriate words as you can think of. For example:

calendar	peace
month	year
independence	future
past	historical
week	history
freedom	laws
famous	liberty
presidents	victory

4. When you are driving, use words such as these in your conversation:

left turn	right turn
north	south
east	west
traffic	transportation
vehicles	urban area
rural area	shopping mall

5. If your family is planning a long-distance trip, hang a map of your state and of the United States near your child's bed. Mark the town in which you live, your destination, and the route you will take to get to your vacation spot. Use as many appropriate words as you can think of. For example:

country	state
city	town
capital	interstate
border	river
lake	

6. Take the map of your itinerary with you. Help your child follow it as you travel.

7. While you are driving on a vacation or trip, use some of these words, if appropriate:

river	creek
stream	lake
ocean	pond
cliff	coast
plains	valley
slope	mountain range
peak	hill
erosion	highway
woods	forest
meadow	pasture
field	quarry
acres	coal mine
cattle	hogs
feeding lot	rural
town	city
urban	village

8. In addition, discuss products made from corn, wheat, soybeans, cotton, wool, milk, trees, oil, and so on.

9. Hang a map of the world near your child's bed. A globe of the world that contains a light bulb makes a wonderful night-light, as well as a learning tool. Use as many appropriate words as you can think of. For example:

country	city
capital	nation
island	sea
ocean	continent
North Pole	South Pole
gulf	trade
boundaries	winds
currents	government
equator	Antarctic
Arctic	

10. Mark on a map countries that are mentioned in the news.

11. Mark on a map the locations where certain products are made.

12. Mark the countries where your ancestors came from. Introduce words like:

ancestors	emigrated
inherited	nationality
citizen	vote
customs	language
memories	Statue of Liberty

TELL YOUR CHILDREN ABOUT THEIR HERITAGE

Many children are interested in their heritage. They like to know about their parents' childhoods and about their grandparents and other relatives. Whether your family has been in this country a long time or they are recent immigrants, their lives are of interest to your children. It is social studies with personal meaning.

Ethnic foods and customs, too, are a wonderful source of vocabulary and information to your child. If you are of ethnic origin and speak the language of your ancestry, don't hesitate to speak that language to your child. A child who has the opportunity to learn a second language at home possesses a skill that less fortunate students spend years in high school and college attempting to acquire. Every aspect of your home life offers opportunities to ask your child thinking questions, to participate in thought-provoking conversations, and to expand your child's vocabulary.

A POOR SOCIAL STUDIES REPORT CARD

Social studies grades cannot be improved overnight. Even if you follow most of the suggestions in this chapter, progress will be gradual. If your child brings home a poor report card in social studies, perhaps a talk with your child's teacher would give you some clues to the problem.

One last note: Don't make every conversation a social studies lesson. Wait for the appropriate occasion and then have a happy, natural conversation.

CHAPTER 5

BETTER GRADES IN SCIENCE

Parents do not have to be scientists in order to help their children get better grades in science. Science is the study of everything around you. If you know about any of the following subjects, you can provide enough information to stimulate your child's curiosity:

weather	the human body
animals	plants
trees	cooking
solar system	fish
flowers	machines
electricity	inventions
water	air
insects	chemicals
heat	rocks
nutrition	diseases
birds	medicines
types of fabrics	family traits
pollution	environment
industrial waste	engines

To make science easier for your child to understand, you only need to talk about what you know. By discussing topics, such as flowers, birds, or the stars, you create an interest and at the same time develop vocabulary. You do not have to teach the topics found in your child's science textbook. The teacher will do that. Instead, indoors or outdoors, do the following:

1. Ask your child to observe objects, such as rocks, clouds, snow, insects, birds, airplanes in flight, balloons, the inside of a flower, shadows, the shape of the moon, lightning and thunder, and so on.

2. Ask your child questions that encourage thinking and curiosity.

3. Be encouraging when your child asks questions.

   For example:

   Kelly: Dad! Look at that pile of ants. What are they doing?

   Dad: Good question, Kelly. Let's watch them for a bit and see what we can find out.

   Kelly: That one is carrying something!

EXAMPLES OF OBJECTS TO OBSERVE AND VOCABULARY TO USE

As a parent, discuss any of the following with your child:

1. A tree in your yard or neighborhood (vocabulary: branches, limbs, trunk, chlorophyll, spreading, roots, bark, sap, gnarl, insect pests, height)

2. How a cat moves (vocabulary: claw, whiskers, intelligence, breed, forefeet, hind feet, padded paws, wild cats, domesticated)

3. The material in your child's clothing (vocabulary: cotton, wool, nylon, synthetic, print, natural, fiber, fabric, textile, woven, silk)

4. Types of materials used in your house and other buildings (vocabulary: brick, steel, wood, aluminum, marble, tinted glass, plastic, stone, concrete, limestone)

5. Clouds on sunny days and rainy days (vocabulary: water vapor, climate, winds, dew, moisture, rain, clouds, fog, atmosphere, space, cloudburst)

6. Pan of water heating (vocabulary: heat, temperature, luke warm, boiling, steam, 212°, evaporating, purifying, bacteria)

7. A seed or cutting from a plant (vocabulary: seedling, cutting, soil, humus, peat moss, fertilizer, bacteria, aphids, insects, insecticide, decay, root)

8. A hand (vocabulary: palm, knuckle, digit, index finger, joint, grasp, fist, grip, extremity, flexible, veins)

9. A picture or model of the human body (vocabulary: organs, liver, kidney, spine, esophagus, stomach, intestines, heart, brain, lungs, jaws, blood, oxygen)

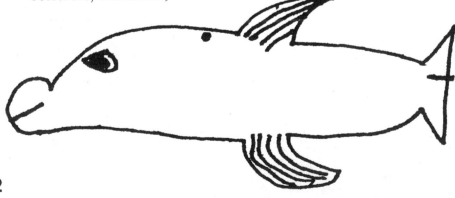

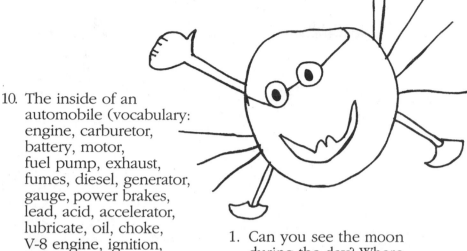

10. The inside of an automobile (vocabulary: engine, carburetor, battery, motor, fuel pump, exhaust, fumes, diesel, generator, gauge, power brakes, lead, acid, accelerator, lubricate, oil, choke, V-8 engine, ignition, plugs, pistons, cylinders, crankshaft, panel)

EXAMPLES OF QUESTIONS TO ASK

As you are talking with your child about different science topics, ask simple open-ended questions that require more than one-word answers. Encourage your child to make observations and to think about both the question and the answer. This is a great opportunity to expand your child's vocabulary. Also encourage your child to ask questions of his or her own. If a child can ask a question about a topic, it often shows that he or she is paying attention and is interested in what is being said. Here are a few examples of possible science questions:

1. Can you see the moon during the day? Where is it? (vocabulary: full moon, crescent moon, lunar, solar, horizon, earth, orbit, sunrise, sunset, eclipse, space)

2. Why are there so many words on the cereal box? (vocabulary: energy, vitamins, ingredients, iron, natural, minerals, fiber, calcium, whole wheat, muscles, cholesterol)

3. Why does bread get moldy? (vocabulary: mold, bacteria, germs, microscope, slide, spoiled, fungus, penicillin, plant)

4. Why does a magnet stick to the refrigerator door? (vocabulary: metal, north and south poles, compass, direction, east, west, north, south)

5. Is a stone living or non-living? Why? (vocabulary: non-living, living, food, movement, growth, reproduce, erosion, senses, death, birth)

6. Why does an apple fall down instead of up? (vocabulary: gravity, weight, weightlessness, Isaac Newton, force, pull, experiment, observe, oxygen, air)

7. Why does milk turn sour? (vocabulary: bacteria, temperature, disease, pasteurize, homogenize, skim, whole milk, cream, germs)

AT WHAT AGE ARE CHILDREN READY FOR SCIENCE?

The earlier parents introduce the world of nature to their children,

learn new words the first time they hear them. It takes many times before they absorb the meanings of some words and concepts.

ONE OF THE BEST USES OF TELEVISION

Nature programs on television, if followed by discussions, are a tremendous help to learning science at home.

The programs provide a variety of interesting, often fascinating, concrete visual images that reinforce the meanings of the science concepts and words.

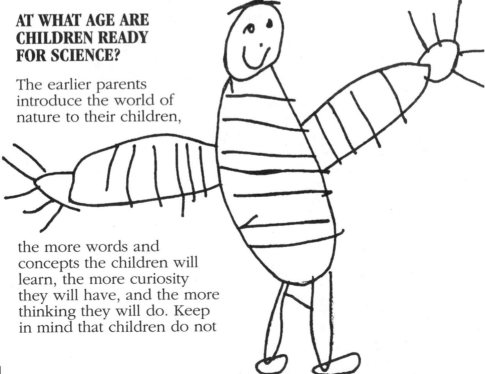

the more words and concepts the children will learn, the more curiosity they will have, and the more thinking they will do. Keep in mind that children do not

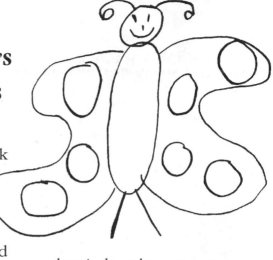

DECORATE YOUR CHILD'S ROOM WITH SCIENCE PICTURES AND POSTERS

Try this experiment after your child has acquired some skill in reading. Tack a poster of the solar system on the wall near your child's bed. You will be surprised at how little time passes before you hear your child using these words: space, star, universe, constellation, planet, galaxy, Milky Way, comet, orbit, Mars, Jupiter, Venus, atmosphere, moons, Uranus, and gravity.

Before long, you'll be asked questions, such as:

"What are the stars made of?"

"What is the Milky Way?"

"What's a galaxy?"

"How did the solar system get here?"

Posters with captions are available at bookstores, museums, and state and national parks on subjects like trees, cats, dogs, horses, trains, airplanes, rockets, ships, butterflies, minerals, gems, flowers, animals, cacti, snakes, minerals, metals, chemicals, solar system, weather, telephones, volcanoes, vitamins, bacteria, rocks, dinosaurs, canyons, simple machines, shells, clocks, dams, and salmon.

COLLECTIONS AND MODELS TEACH SCIENCE, TOO

Many children like to collect a variety of objects, including items they find and those that they buy. Children who collect things often develop specialized vocabularies that often exceed the vocabularies of their parents and teachers. Even six-year-olds can develop amazing vocabularies through their collections of dinosaur models, airplane models, shells, and so on.

SHOULD I BUY SCIENCE BOOKS FOR MY CHILD?

Answer: Yes. Bookstores have beautiful science books for children of all ages. Supermarkets and discount stores, too, have attractive, authoritative science books for children on a variety of subjects. It is important, however, to choose books that are of interest to your child. Many science books have vocabularies that may be above your child's reading level. Children who are encouraged to pursue their interests in science develop large vocabularies, as well as read and understand material that is often above their current reading levels. If a book is too difficult for your child, he or she will let you know. Your child will either seem frustrated or show little interest in the material.

Encyclopedias are also wonderful resources to have around for answering questions, especially when parents and children look up answers together. You don't have to know science to teach your child a variety of important science concepts. What information you don't know, you can find out together. Every science concept learned at home will help your child be better prepared for science at school.

CHAPTER 6
HELPING YOUR CHILD BECOME
A BETTER COMMUNICATOR

SOME CHILDREN ARE BORN COMMUNICATORS, OTHERS ARE MADE

In today's world, successful people are good communicators. They must communicate their ideas to other people through words. For some, it's a natural talent; for others, it's an acquired skill. In either case, the time to begin teaching children to communicate effectively is when they are young. Children are practicing communication all the time through interaction with their parents, siblings, and playmates—when they play games, through conversations, writing stories, and so on. Children need to be able to comfortably express their ideas, thoughts, and opinions in order to communicate.

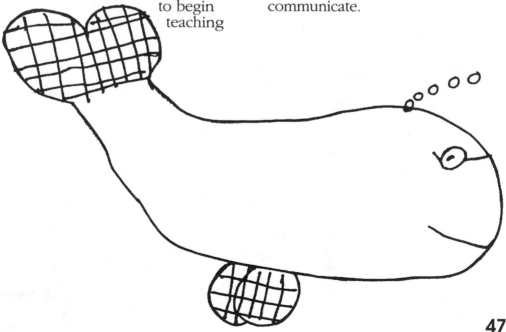

THE NEED FOR KNOWING HOW TO COMMUNICATE

In most classrooms, there are going to be some children who do not know how to adequately express themselves. They may feel threatened by another child, confused about what they are supposed to do, or feel ill and not able to describe their symptoms. They are unaccustomed to describing what is troubling them. Sometimes it is easier to hit another child or cry instead of asking for help.

In the classroom, children need to understand their teacher's explanations, assignments, and directions. In turn, children must learn to answer the teacher's questions, express their own thoughts, ask questions, and communicate with other children.

WRITTEN COMMUNICATION

Children begin creative writing in school very early. Often, in kindergarten, children are writing short stories with the help of an adult. As children grow older, they continue their writing. They begin to write essays, reports, letters, and so on. Writing is a wonderful activity for organizing thoughts and expressing opinions or relating facts.

To help improve your child's communication skills, encourage keeping a journal and writing letters to friends and family. Don't be concerned about spelling at this point. The goal is for

your child to write for
pleasure, freely and without
criticism. The more your
child writes, the better he
or she will become at this
skill. Let your child know
how delighted you are
with his or her writing and
the writing will continue
and improve.

CHAPTER 7

● ● ● ● ● ● ● ● ● ● ● ● ● ● ● ● ● ● ●

GAMES TO IMPROVE LANGUAGE
AND THINKING SKILLS

The games presented here can be played while you are preparing dinner, riding in your car, or waiting to be served in a restaurant. All are designed to develop language and thinking skills. You are one of the players. When it is your turn to present a word or words, use at least one word that your child does not know. This will encourage your child to ask "What does that word mean?"

❤ RIDDLE TIME ❤

How to Play

Use three or more sentences to describe a person, place, or thing. Your child guesses what you are describing. Take time to discuss the answer, if necessary. Offer a point for every correct guess. Then it is your child's turn to present three sentences. Your sentences should be difficult to answer,

but not so difficult as to be discouraging. There isn't a specific age range for this game. You can play this game with a child as young as 3 or 4, as long as the item you select is familiar. Once you start playing, you'll know what adjustments you need to make so that your child is successful and learning new words at the same time.

Example

It is a book.
It contains many words.
It helps you spell words.
You can find word definitions and antonyms and synonyms in it.

Comments

"Dictionary," of course, is the answer. Note that the advanced words "antonym" and "synonym" were used. Six-year-olds can learn these words, too. Your introduction of these words at an early age will be valuable when they are later taught in school.

Variation

Supply three possible answers to your statements. For example: telephone book, dictionary, book of

poems. Your child chooses the correct answer. This makes the game easier. It is also a good time to talk about the differences between a telephone book and a dictionary.

❤ SILLY TIME ❤

How to Play

Make two statements about something in the house, shopping center, outdoors, and so on. One statement is silly; the other appropriate. Your child decides which is which. This game is appropriate for ages 3 to 10. The vocabulary you choose will determine the level of difficulty of the game.

Example

The chair is tiny and timid. The sofa is comfortable and attractive.

Comments

The first sentence, of course, is the silly one. The more ridiculous you make the sentences, the more your child will like them. A brief discussion should follow as to why one sentence is silly and the other is not. Your child will learn that inappropriate words sound silly.

❤ DO NOT TOUCH ❤

How to Play

As you walk through various stores or outdoor places, ask your child to describe how an item you see might feel. Ask your child to describe the object without touching it. This is a good opportunity to introduce new and unfamiliar words. This game is especially appropriate for children ages 3 to 8, although it can be played with older children, too.

Examples

rough	choppy
jagged	velvety
scratchy	ruffled
rocky	silky
soft	bumpy
stony	smooth
sharp	woolly
spongy	prickly
hairy	satiny
fluffy	moist
flimsy	mushy
feathery	crisp

Comments

Many of the words your child learns through this game many appear in the stories he or she later reads at school. Reading is much more enjoyable when readers have a mental picture of the objects described. Through this simple game, you can add many new words to your child's vocabulary. You can also play the same game allowing your child to touch the objects.

❤ CLASSIFICATION TIME ❤

How to Play

Ask your child to name some words that apply to a specific object—a tank truck, for example. Correct responses might include milk, gasoline, oil, liquids, chemicals, oxygen, poisonous gases, fuel, and so on.

Examples

A pair of (shoes, scissors, pants, glasses)
A dozen (eggs, doughnuts, ears of corn)

A bowl of (cereal, fruit, cherries, soup, flowers)
A pail of (cement, water, sand, dirt, slop)
A pound of (coffee, butter, (hamburger, peanuts)
A group of (children, houses, automobiles, boats)
A set of (dishes, chairs, china, silverware)

Comments

Classification skills are important at any age. Begin as soon as your child is old enough to understand what you are asking him or her to do. Continue with more

difficult words as long as your child still enjoys the game. Often, children know words in one context, but they are confused when the words are used in another situation. Children will understand "Would you set the table, please?" but they may be mystified if the teacher talks about a "set" of numbers.

❤ WORD BUILDING ❤

How to Play

Say a word. Then ask your child to think of another word that could be added to it to make a new and longer word. Say the word "bed," for example. Your child might respond with bedroom, bedtime story, or bedspread.

Examples

any	some	no	every
with	body	high	by
road	way	in	be
side	mail	work	fire
foot	head	under	wear
table	tea	blue	black
cross	book	side	over
hand	foot	meat	night

Comments

This game introduces children to compound words. Recognizing and understanding the meanings of compound words is an important skill in learning to read.

❤ OCCUPATIONS ❤

How to Play

Here is another easy game to keep your child busy as you are working about the house or as a bedtime activity. Name an occupation, such as farmer or dentist. Ask your child to name some tools or other objects a farmer or dentist might need to carry out his or her work (plow, cultivator, harvester, drill, x-rays, dental floss).

Examples

truck driver	doctor
waitress	musician
barber	superintendent
reporter	cook
engineer	football player
secretary	pharmacist
dentist	principal
artist	manufacturer
florist	veterinarian
carpenter	plumber
pilot	

Comments

This game provides an excellent opportunity to extend your child's vocabulary. Give "points" for a certain number of responses or for a particularly good word. Later, your child can trade in points for a small reward.

❤ TWO FOR ONE ❤

How to Play

This game is best for children ages 6 to 10. Ask your child to name two words that sound alike, yet have different meanings, such as "blue" and "blew." You might want to give "points" for each correct set of words.

Examples

piece, peace	flower, flour
ate, eight	site, sight, cite
made, maid	foul, fowl
waist, waste	course, coarse
weak, week	idol, idle, idyll
rain, reign	night, knight
plain, plane	fourth, forth
to, two, too	which, witch

Comments

A casual discussion of homophones (words that sound the same, but are spelled differently and have different meanings) will later help your child's reading comprehension and spelling.

❤ FOLLOW THE DIRECTIONS ❤

How to Play

Hide an object, such as an Easter egg, snack, birthday present or balloon, in your house or in a room in which you are working. Give directions for finding the object, such as walk three paces north; walk to the right side of the room; now, walk to the opposite side of the room. Use the directional words listed on page 57 and others that you can think of. Children who are four-years-old can understand straight ahead, backwards, sideways, and so on. Left, right, north, south, east, and west are more appropriate for older children.

Examples

south	west
backward	sideways
forward	rear
right	left
directly across	north
straight ahead	east
clockwise	foot
right-angle turn	yard
counterclockwise	

Comments

Give at least five directions to help locate the object. You may give three directions at once to help develop memory skills. This game also develops a sense of direction and the ability to follow directions.

❤ TRUE DEFINITIONS ❤

How to Play

Team A (this is a family or party game) gives Team B a word. Each member of Team A gives a definition of the word they have presented. Some definitions may be silly, some inaccurate, but one definition must be correct. As each member of Team A presents his or her definition, he or she must try to

convince Team B that the definition is the correct one. Team B has one chance to decide which definition is correct. Team A continues offering new words until Team B makes a correct guess. Then it is Team B's turn. This game is best for ages 6 and up.

Comments

For this game, a dictionary may be necessary. The difficulty of the word to be defined should be adjusted to the ability of the players. The game works best when there are three or more players on each team.

❤ IF I GAVE YOU ❤ THREE THINGS

How to Play

Say to your child: If I gave you three objects (for example, a notebook, a portfolio, and a pencil), which one would you return? What would you do with the other two? Have your child explain the choices he or she is willing to make. At least one of the objects should be a word your child does not know, thus providing an opportunity for your child to learn new words. Afterwards, it is your child's turn to suggest three items.

Examples

a piece of chalk, a box of vitamins, a tumbler

a picture frame, a skillet, an eggplant

a bottle of glue, bacteria, a microscope

a comb, some purple dye, a bale of cotton

a pearl, a diamond, a ruby

a flying carpet, a gold pen, a velvet robe

a chicken, a pheasant, a coop

Comments

This game can be made more difficult by asking that the two items kept by your child be used in a

sentence. For example:
The pencil can be used to write in the notebook. The vitamins can be swallowed with water in a tumbler.

❤ I'LL GIVE YOU ❤ A POINT

How to Play

Challenge your child to find a new word in a television commercial or program that he or she is watching. Have your child write the word down, helping with the spelling if necessary. After the program is over, discuss the meaning of the word using a dictionary. Then ask your child to use the word correctly in a sentence during the next half hour. Give "points" if he or she uses the word correctly. If you wish, points can be redeemed for a small reward, such as a sticker.

Comments

This game not only develops your child's vocabulary, but encourages your child to listen carefully as well.

CHAPTER 8

· · · · · · · · · · · · · · · · · ·

VOCABULARY INTRODUCED
BY CATEGORIES

This section provides a variety of vocabulary words to introduce to children between the ages of three and ten. The words are arranged by categories. When you know you are going to an athletic event or the zoo, for example, you can take a look at the list to see which word or words you would like to introduce to your child. You might also want to glance through the lists when you have a moment so you will have some vocabulary words in mind when an opportunity presents itself.

ATHLETICS

amusement	arena	athlete	bout
competition	competitor	contention	contest
contestant	course	court	daring
entertainment	equipment	even	excel
field	foe	gallant	gear
opponent	oppose	opposition	par
participant	recreation	referee	rival
rivalry	score	spectator	stadium

CELEBRATIONS

anniversary	bravery	ceremony	commemorate
country	courage	festival	festivities
gala	gathering	harvest	holiday
honor	honorable	independence	jamboree

joyful Labor Day Lincoln loyalty
memorial Memorial Day New Year's Day observance
occasion occurrence outing pageant
peace reception rejoice rites

DOCTORS AND DENTISTS

ailment analyze appointment check-up
clinic comfortable conference crisis
delicate emergency examination fitness
frail harmful health heart
hygiene hygienic infirmity injurious
observe operation oral probe
progress robust sample specimen
sterile stethoscope stomach suffer
surgery vitality waiting room X-ray

EATING IN, EATING OUT

appetite appetizing beneficial broil
cafeteria calcium carbohydrates carve
consume edible etiquette feast
gulp healthful hearty inedible
ingredients iron liquid luncheon
manners minerals natural nourishing
nutrients poached polite protein
ravenous refreshments relish restaurant
roasted rude solids tart
tasty unappetizing vitamins wholesome
whole wheat

FAMILY AND FUN

adolescent	adult	aging	anniversary
bride	clownish	comedy	comical
droll	enjoy	entertaining	farcical
frolic	generation	groom	heirlooms
household	humorous	immature	in-laws
infancy	jolly	juvenile	laughable
ludicrous	maiden name	maternal	mature
mirth	offspring	oldest, eldest	outlandish
paternal	rejoice	relatives	relax
reunion	ridiculous	siblings	witty

GARDENING

agriculture	annuals	aphids	seedlings
begonias	bulbs	bone meal	chrysanthemums
cultivate	deciduous	edger	evergreen
fertilizer	fungus	harvest	hazard
hedge	hoe	insecticide	ivy
litter	mulch	perennials	vegetation

HOUSES

apartment	brass	carpeting	cement
china	colonial	concrete	cottage
decorate	draperies	dwelling	electrical
fiberglass	fixture	furnishings	hinge
household	inhabit	insulation	linoleum

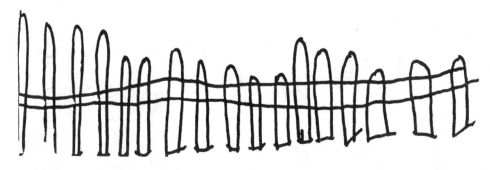

lumber
molding
plumbing
polish
porcelain
possessions
radiator
ranch house
resident
split-level
stain
tenant
highrise
thermopane
varnish
wallboard

INVENTIONS

advanced
amplifier
antenna
atomic energy
automatic
cable
calculator
cash register
chisel
clarinet
complex
computer
conceive
create
creator
design
detailed
devise
digital
electronic
fabricate
hatch
imaginative
improve
ingenuity
instrument
inventor
jack
manual
mechanical
missile
original
originate
pioneer
pump
rocket
software
technology
telescope
microscope

JOBS

admiral
astronaut
artist
assistant
author
editor
business
career
clerk
craft
curator
custodian
customer
electrician
employee
employment
engineer
foreman
hostess
illustrator

inspector	laborer	lawyer	librarian
mayor	maintenance	operator	occupation
pharmacist	plumber	president	profession
programmer	reporter	salesperson	secretary
specialist	superintendent	unemployed	veterinarian

KITCHEN

aluminum	aroma	bake	boil
broil	colander	condiment	container
cork	counter	degrees	flavor
fry	gallon	kettle	light fixture
medium	microwave	one-fourth	one-half
one-third	ounce	pantry	pint
poach	pound	produce	quart
rare	scrape	sift	simmer
skillet	spatula	stainless steel	strainer
switch	temperature	utensil	whip

LIVELY

alive	amiable	animated	brisk
bouncy	buoyant	dynamic	eager
enchanting	energetic	enthusiastic	fancy
intense	interesting	keen	peppery
radiant	spirited	vigorous	vital

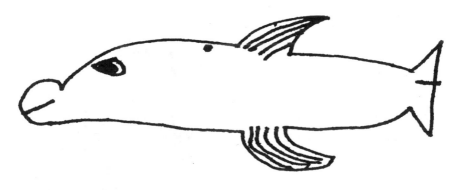

MONEY

amount	assets
balance	capital
cash	dime
dollar	income
penny	quarter
riches	savings
salary	treasure
wealth	wealthy

NEW

contemporary	current	latest
modern	original	past
present	recent	unexplored
untested	untried	

NEWS

advertise	announcement	article
bulletin	circulate	dispatch
gossip	information	intelligence
rumor		

NOISE

buzz	chatter	clatter
commotion	disturbance	humming
laughter	outcry	racket
uproar		

ODD

eerie
unusual
extraordinary
outlandish

OFF

cancel
conclude
disconnected
incorrect

ON

commence
evolve
proceed
progress

OPEN

ajar
unfasten
unfolding
unobstructed

PRAISE

abundant	amuse	applaud	astonishing
awesome	charm	cheer	commend
compliment	convincing	delight	enchant
fantastic	flatter	impressive	laud
mighty	miraculous	potent	remarkable
skilled	superior	supreme	wondrous

QUICK

accelerate	brisk	fleet	hasty
immediately	instantly	leap	mobile
nimble	prompt	pronto	rapid

TRAVEL

avenue	boulevard	by-pass	commute
cruise	descend	detour	expedition
itinerary	jaunt	journey	kilometer
lane	luggage	passage	pounce
roam	route	transportation	tour

UPS AND DOWNS

angry	annoy	appreciate	blissful
bully	carefree	cheerful	concerned
confusion	content	delighted	ecstatic
enjoyed	false	fret	generous
gloomy	irritate	jealous	jovial
jubilant	miserable	pleasant	rewarding
rude	saddened	satisfying	worry

VISITING CITIES

capital	factory	fair	gallery
hotel	industries	institute	market
mayor	metropolis	municipality	skyscraper
spectacle	stadium	structure	subway
train			

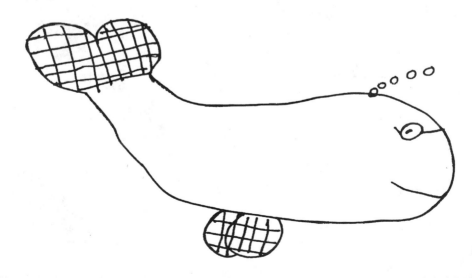

WEATHER

arctic	arid	atmosphere	balmy
brutal	biting	blast	breeze
calm	chilly	climate	cozy
dew	draft	dry spell	drench
drizzle	fog	freezing point	frigid
frost	glacial	glow	gust
hail	heat wave	humid	hurricane
mild	moisture	parched	piercing
raw	temperate	temperature	tornado
torrid	tranquil	tropical	wintry

YEARS

annual	biennial
century	current
date	familiar
immediately	future
latest	latter
modern	modernized
once	present
recent	recreate
refresh	remodel
restore	revive
timely	

YESTERYEARS

ancient	antique
dated	eternal
everlasting	historic
history	infinite
obsolete	olden

old-fashioned   original   past   preceding
prehistoric   previous   primitive   restored
yesterday

ZOO

animal kingdom   barrier   beak   boundary
civilized   confined   coop   creature
domestic   domesticated   duckling   enclose
enclosure   endangered   extinct   ferocious
fierce   flecked   fleecy   game
hibernate   mammal   menagerie   molting
native   natural   non-human   nurse
pen   railing   restrict   restrain
rodent   savage   separate   shelter
species   speckled   striped   tusk

CHAPTER 9
SYNONYM DICTIONARY FOR PARENTS

The entries in this dictionary contain words an adult will commonly use. The synonyms are probably familiar to you as well. Be aware that some of the words may be only loosely synonymous. Pick out one or two new words to use each day when talking to your child. Then watch your child's vocabulary grow!

A

ability - expertise, talent
able - capable, competent
accept - approve, tolerate
accident - calamity, mishap
adjust - adapt, conform
agree - concur, consent
aid - assist, support
alike - comparable, similar
all - entire, total
almost - approximately, nearly
alone - solitary, solo
always - constantly, continuously
amuse - entertain, delight

anger - enrage, infuriate
angry - aggravated, irate
animal - beast, creature
annoy - bother, disturb
answer - reply, respond
apart - detached, isolated
argue - debate, dispute
ask - inquire, request
avoid - evade, shun
awful - dreadful, horrible

B

baby - infant, toddler
back - hind, rear
bad - disagreeable, rotten
beach - coast, shore
battle - clash, contest
bawl - howl, wail
beautiful - handsome, splendid
before - earlier, previously
beg - implore, plead
behavior - conduct, demeanor
below - beneath, underneath
belt - band, sash
bend - curve, hook
best - excel, triumph

better - superior, surpass
bite - chomp, gnaw
blame - criticize, denounce
block - bar, impede
bloom - blossom, flower
boil - bubble, simmer
bright - brilliant, radiant

C

car - automobile, vehicle
care - concern, worry
careful - cautious, considerate
careless - heedless, thoughtless
carry - lug, tote
catch - capture, grasp
center - core, middle
change - alter, modify
chase - follow, pursue
cheerful - buoyant, sunny
child - juvenile, youngster
childish - immature, infantile
chilly - frosty, nippy
choose - elect, select
city - municipality, town
clean - immaculate, unsoiled
clear - cloudless, transparent

D

dainty - delicate, exquisite
damage - blemish, mar
damp - moist, wet
danger - hazard, risk
dangerous - risky, treacherous
dark - dim, murky
darling - adorable, delightful
dawn - daybreak, sunrise
dead - deceased, departed
deed - achievement, feat
defeat - overthrow, rout

defend - guard, shield
delay - retard, slow
delightful - pleasing, pleasurable
demand - compel, require
deny - contradict, withhold
describe - depict, explain
destroy - demolish, wreck
different - dissimilar, unlike
dip - dunk, submerge
dishonest - deceitful, untruthful
dislike - aversion, prejudice
disturb - agitate, upset
do - perform, complete
done - completed, finished
drag - haul, lug
dry - arid, waterless

E

eager - keen, impatient
earth - globe, world
easy - effortless, simple
eat - consume, devour
edge - border, margin
empty - bare, vacant
end - close, conclusion

enemy - foe, opponent
energy - power, vigor
enjoy - appreciate, relish
enough - adequate, sufficient
entire - complete, whole
equal - equivalent, identical
equip - furnish, outfit
erase - cancel, delete
error - mistake, slip
escape - breakout, flight
evening - dusk, nightfall
evil - harmful, wicked
excuse - alibi, pardon
extra - excess, surplus

F

fail - decline, weaken
fair - impartial, just
fake - pretend, sham
fall - topple, tumble
false - deceptive, untrue
family - folk, kin
famous - noted, prominent
fancy - elaborate, intricate
far - distant, outlying
fast - rapid, swift
fat - obese, stout
fault - blame, guilt
fear - alarm, fright
feel - handle, touch
few - handful, scattering
fight - battle, scuffle
filthy - dirty, squalid
fine - excellent, superior
finish - complete, conclude
firm - secure, solid
first - initial, primary
fit - proper, suitable
fix - overhaul, repair

flat - even, level
fly - flit, flutter
foolish - absurd, wacky
forgive - excuse, pardon
fortune - riches, wealth
free - loose, unconfined
full - brimming, crammed
funny - comic, laughable

G

gentle - mild, soothing
gloomy - bleak, depressing
gain - achieve, attain
gather - assemble, collect
general - typical, usual
gentle - mild, tender

get - acquire, obtain
giant - gigantic, huge
give - contribute, donate
glad - delighted, joyful
gloomy - dejected, melancholy
go - advance, proceed
gone - departed, vanished
good - beneficial, favorable
great - outstanding, superior
group - assemble, cluster
guard - protect, shield
guide - conduct, escort

H

handy - convenient, useful
happy - contented, joyful
hard - firm, solid
harden - stiffen, solidify
harmful - damaging, injurious
hate - detest, loath
haul - lug, tow
healthy - robust, thriving
heavy - hefty, massive
help - assist, support
hide - bury, conceal
hike - tramp, trek
hit - strike, whack
hold - reserve, retain
hop - bounce, spring
hopeful - expectant, optimistic
hot - sultry, torrid
huge - colossal, gigantic
humor - comedy, wit
hurt - abuse, damage

I

icy - freezing, frigid
idea - notion, thought
illness - ailment, infirmity
imagine - suppose, visualize
immediately - directly, instantly
improve - correct, rectify
increase - augment, expand
innocent - blameless, guiltless
inspect - examine, survey
irritate - aggravate, exasperate

J

jab - nudge, prod
jam - fix, scrape
job - chore, duty
join - connect, link
jolly - gleeful, jovial
joyful - buoyant, effervescent
jump - leap, spring

K

keep - retain, withhold
kick - boot, wallop
kid - youngster, youth
know - comprehend, grasp

L

large - immense, vast
last - concluding, final
late - overdue, tardy

later - afterward, subsequently
laugh - chuckle, titter
lean - slope, tilt
leave - depart, exit
lie - falsify, fib
lift - elevate, hoist
like - admire, approve
little - miniscule, petite
long - extended, lengthy
look - gaze, peer
loose - relaxed, unrestrained
lose - forfeit, misplace
lost - irretrievable, missing
lot - abundance, heap
love - adore, cherish
lump - chunk, wad
lying - deceitful, dishonest

M

mad - furious, irate
make - create, produce
many - numerous, various
match - duplicate, equal
meal - fare, spread
melt - liquefy, thaw
mend - patch, repair
mess - botch, bungle
mild - balmy, gentle
miss - disregard, overlook
mistake - error, blunder
mix - blend, combine
more - additional, greater
morning - dawn, daybreak
move - march, proceed
much - exceedingly, plenty
museum - exhibition, gallery

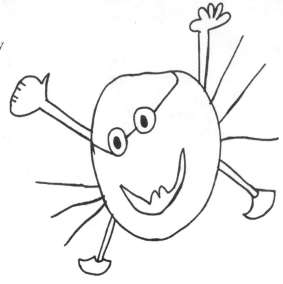

N

nag - harass, hound
nap - slumber, snooze
nasty - offensive, vile
near - beside, close
need - desire, requirement
neglect - disregard, ignore
nervous - agitated, edgy
new - fresh, recent
next - ensuing, following
nice - agreeable, pleasing
night - dusk, evening
noisy - racket, uproarious
nonsense - bosh, gibberish
notice - heed, observe
now - immediately, instantly
number - digit, numeral
nutritious - healthy, nourishing

O

obey - comply, conform
observe - perceive, view

odd - curious, peculiar
offer - extend, present
often - frequently, repeatedly
old - aged, ancient
only - sole, unique
open - ajar, unlocked
opinion - belief, view
order - arrange, organize
ordinary - routine, usual

P

pain - ache, distress
part - fraction, section
past - former, prior
path - track, trail
pay - compensate, reimburse
perfect - flawless, unblemished
pest - annoyance, nuisance
pick - choose, select
plain - modest, simple
pleasant - agreeable, pleasing
plenty - abundant, ample
praise - applaud, compliment
pretty - attractive, beautiful
prevent - anticipate, forestall
prior - earlier, preceding
promise - pledge, vow
promote - advance, elevate
proper - applicable, suitable
protect - defend, guard
punish - correct, discipline
push - propel, shove
puzzle - mystery, bewilder

Q

qualified - capable, competent
quarrel - argument, dispute
quench - extinguish, satisfy
question - inquire, quiz
quick - rapid, swift
quiet - hushed, silent

R

rage - fury, wrath
raise - elevate, hoist
real - authentic, genuine
reduce - decrease, diminish
reject - eliminate, exclude
relate - describe, recite
relieve - alleviate, ease
remark - comment, mention
repair - reconstruct, overhaul
replace - restore, reinstate
report - narrate, recount
rest - recline, relax
rich - affluent, wealthy
rid - abolish, exterminate
ride - excursion, tour
right - exact, precise
rim - border, edge
ripe - mature, mellow
risky - hazardous, perilous
roar - bellow, clamor
rock - sway, quake
roll - rotate, revolve
rub - chafe, scrape
ruin - demolish, destroy
rule - law, ordinance
run - dash, sprint
rush - hurry, race

S

sack - container, pouch
sad - dejected, depressed
safe - intact, unharmed
sag - slip, slide
same - exact, identical
sassy - impertinent, insolent
save - conserve, sustain
say - declare, utter
scare - alarm, startle
scatter - disperse, spread
scold - berate, reprimand
score - record, tally

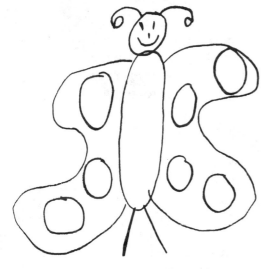

scrape - grate, scuff
scream - screech, shriek
scrub - cleanse, scour
seam - bond, joint
search - rummage, scour
secret - confidential, covert
see - notice, observe
seek - hunt, search
send - dispatch, ship
serious - grave, solemn

settle - conclude, resolve
several - sundry, various
sharp - honed, keen
shine - beam, radiate
short - brief, abbreviated
show - display, exhibit
shy - bashful, timid
sick - ill, unwell
silent - mum, mute
silly - flighty, giddy
simple - modest, unpretentious
sing - carol, serenade
size - measurement, dimension
skill - expertise, knack
slide - glide, slither
slim - slender, thin
sloppy - slovenly, untidy
slow - unhurried, plodding
smart - bright, brilliant
smell - odor, scent
smile - beam, grin
smooth - even, flat
smudge - smear, soil
soak - drench, saturate
soil - dirt, earth
solve - clarify, settle
soon - presently, shortly
sorry - regretful, remorseful
speed - hustle, rush
splash - douse, splatter
split - divide, sever
start - begin, commence
stick - adhere, cling
stop - cease, halt
strike - assault, attack
strong - mighty, powerful
succeed - prosper, thrive
suggestion - idea, proposal
surprise - amaze, astonish

T

task - chore, duty
tasteful - flavorful, savory
teach - educate, instruct
tell - declare, relate
terrible - appalling, dreadful
terror - dread, panic
thankful - appreciative, grateful
thin - slender, slight
things - belongings, possessions
think - imagine, ponder
throw - fling, hurl
ticket - label, tag
tight - constricted, taut
tiny - diminutive, miniature
tire - exhaust, fatigue
too - additionally, also
toss - cast, lob
total - complete, entire
touch - finger, handle
treasure - cherish, value
treat - morsel, tidbit
tremble - quiver, shudder
trick - prank, ruse
trouble - concern, distress
trust - confidence, faith
try - attempt, endeavor
tumble - plunge, topple

U

ugly - hideous, unsightly
unbending - inflexible, rigid
uncommon - unusual, infrequent
unconcerned - indifferent, aloof
uncovered - bare, exposed
undamaged - flawless, intact
under - below, beneath
understand - comprehend, grasp
uneasy - edgy, tense
uneven - irregular, lopsided
unfair - inequitable, unjust
unhappy - melancholy, saddened
unhurt - intact, sound
unite - join, link
unsafe - hazardous, risky
unsure - doubtful, dubious
unthinking - heedless, rash
unwell - ailing, indisposed
upset - disarray, muddle
urge - prod, spur
use - apply, employ

V

vacation - holiday, leave
vast - gigantic, huge
view - examine, inspect

W

wacky - absurd, balmy
wad - chunk, clump
wait - linger, remain
waken - arouse, stir
walk - saunter, stroll
wander - drift, meander
want - crave, desire
warn - alert, caution
waste - fritter, squander
watch - scan, scrutinize
way - path, route
weak - feeble, frail
weary - drained, fatigued

weird - eerie, peculiar
well - correctly, properly
wet - drench, saturate
wicked - evil, sinful
wild - unruly, untamed
windy - blustery, gusty
wise - insightful, sage
wonderful - amazing, marvelous
work - employment, occupation
worry - concern, fret
wrap - enclose, envelop
wreck - demolish, destroy
wrong - erroneous, untrue

X Y Z

yield - relinquish, surrender
young - callow, immature
zesty - pungent, snappy

FUN BOOKS TO READ WITH YOUR CHILD

Anna's Garden Songs by Mary Q. Steele

Beezus and Ramona by Beverly Cleary

Bread and Jam for Frances by Russell Hoban

Charlie and the Chocolate Factory by Roald Dahl

Chicka Chicka Boom Boom by Bill Martin, Jr.

Curious George by H. A. Rey

Egyptian Cinderella by Ruth Heller

The Giving Tree by Shel Silverstein

Hattie and the Fox by Mem Fox

Jumanji by Chris Van Allsburg

A Light in the Attic by Shel Silverstein

Lion, the Witch, and the Wardrobe by C. S. Lewis

My Dog Is Lost by Ezra Jack Keats

Red Riding Hood by Beatrice Schenk De Regniers

The Secret Garden by Frances Hodgson Burnett

Yertle the Turtle and Other Stories by Dr. Seuss